Cottage Country

Cottage Country

TEXT BY PAUL KING
PHOTOGRAPHS BY DUDLEY WITNEY

B. Mitchell

Photograph on page 1:
**Nothing so formal as
a frame to hold this
ancient photograph in
place on the living
room wall.**

Photograph on pages 2-3:
**The cottages are
dwarfed by trees,
near Nottawasaga
Beach, Georgian Bay.**

Photograph on page 4:
**A selection of fly rods
and reels.**

Produced by Discovery Books for SMITHBOOKS
113 Merton Street
Toronto, Ontario
M4S 1A8

ISBN 0 88665 945 0

Printed and bound in Hong Kong

91 92 93 94 95 6 5 4 3 2 1

Contents

Wood, Water and Stone

The massive rocks are a place for sunning and swimming at High Falls, on the Muskoka River.

Cottage Country!

The phrase is as cosily familiar to most Canadians as maple syrup, corn roast or Indian Summer. Yet to much of the world it's unknown. Russia has its birch-shaded dachas, Spain its stucco haciendas, China its lily-pond gazebos, Switzerland its alpine chalets, Britain its seaside resorts - but they don't call their summer spas "cottage country." The expression is almost exclusively Canadian.

To us, it evokes an image of towering pines and blue-green waterways, of sleek mahogany boats and weathered cedar docks, of wimpering loons and red sunsets. It also embodies a state of mind, an environment of serene escape. No fax machines, no traffic growl, no deadlines. A place where the smell of woodsmoke replaces smog.

In this land so vast, the second largest on earth, with dense forest tracts sweeping between two seas, cottages have become part of the twentieth century scene. There are cabins in Newfoundland coves, mansions along the St. Lawrence River and sprawling A-frames in the Rockies, but the quintessential cottage country is Muskoka, that rocky, rolling summer paradise in Ontario, which embraces 1,600 lakes and seventeen rivers within its 1,500 square miles.

It was here that the Hurons and Algonquins fished and hunted in the summer, and here where the earliest European set foot in Ontario. He was the first of the fabled *coureurs de bois*, the nineteen-year-old Frenchman Etienne Brulé, who was sent by the explorer Samuel de Champlain in 1610 to live with the chiefs of both tribes for two years. This buckskin-clad adventurer, who later became the first European to see lakes Ontario, Huron, Erie and Superior, lived among the Muskoka Indians for much of his life - until finally he was murdered by the natives whom he idolized.

Samuel de Champlain himself paddled through the north to Muskoka's shores in the summer of 1615, followed swiftly by zealous groups of Frenchmen in search of pelts and souls. For more than three decades fur traders and priests set up traplines and missions in Muskoka, until, in the spring of 1648, the Iroquois suddenly attacked. In the wake of the savage slaughter, the Huron and Algonquin nations were nearly annihilated.

By the end of the century, French traders had again slipped across Muskoka's borders, and explorers were charting its rivers. This was despite the terms of the Treaty of Paris, ratified in 1763, by which Canada passed from French to British rule. Muskoka, meanwhile, was claimed by the Chippewa nation from whose chief, Mesquakie, it took its name.

At the end of the American revolution, white settlers - including the United Empire Loyalists - started swarming in from the south. The government asked Mesquakie to guarantee their safety. But what it really wanted was his land for white settlement. And this it achieved with stunning success. In slightly more than three decades, the Chippewas forfeited by treaty nearly four million acres of land, from Georgian Bay to Haliburton. When Mesquakie later begged for land on which to cultivate crops, he was sold 1,600 acres at Rama on Lake Couchiching for $3,200. Other Chippewas were placed on reserves. During the border crisis of 1836 the British conscripted them all into service.

And still, the treaties were signed. By 1856, the Chippewas had surrendered most of their islands in lakes Simcoe, Couchiching and Georgian

Previous pages: In fast boats young people head for the bow to enjoy the bounce and the spray.

On every dock there is a chair from which to watch the always-changing water.

Bay. As the settlers and squatters poured into the region, the Indians continued pressing claims for unsurrendered land. It wasn't until 1923 that the government finally paid compensation - five years after the First World War.

It was more than two centuries after Etienne Brulé's arrival that Europeans took over Muskoka. But maps and surveys of the land so rich in wildlife had been kept from the beginning. One was Champlain's own map of 1632. Another in 1656 shows Muskoka's main lakes and Indian bands. A third shows Lake Muskoka as one of the chief sources of beaver traded to the Dutch and English. But not until Britain faced war with the States did her soldiers begin surveying Muskoka's waterways with a vengeance.

By the late 1780s, army engineers had charted routes from Toronto to Severn River and across to Georgian Bay. At the end of the War of 1812 surveyors were mapping Muskoka. Yet it wasn't until 1826 that Lieutenant Henry Briscoe of the Royal Engineers not only crossed Muskoka to the Lake of Bays (becoming the first European to do so), but he also found a route to the Ottawa River.

Still, the main exploration of the region was left to David Thompson, the famed explorer of the Columbia River. In 1837, at the age of sixty-seven, he surveyed the three main Muskoka lakes and traced its major rivers, before going on to map the Lake of Bays. From his handwritten records came the first exact maps of Muskoka's waterways. But he made one major error. He grossly over-estimated the land fit for cultivation along the Muskoka River. He reckoned it amounted to 1,024,000 acres - which would have allowed 200 acres apiece to 5,120 families. At a time when Upper Canada's population had spiraled to 400,000, hopes of a northern farm belt were instantly fired.

Though other surveyors warned of Muskoka's "great abundance of Rocks," the Legislature ignored them. It desperately wanted settlers in the north, and started building roads. The trails soon ran from Washago into Gravenhurst and Bracebridge - then on to Port Carling, and Huntsville in the north. Because of the forest swamps, most were built of split pine logs laid side by side with the flat side down. The settlers called them "corduroy roads," but most were rutted lanes of mud. Still, the stagecoaches clattered over them from Orillia, bringing rib-bruised new settlers from the Old World. Under the Free Grants and Homestead Act, any family head could select 200 acres, provided he built a house and cultivated fifteen acres within five years. To the land-hungry poor of Europe the Act was a godsend. Within two decades from 1871, Muskoka's population swelled from just over 5,000 to nearly 16,000.

Some mined, some trapped, and the foolhardy farmed the rocks. The smart ones turned to lumbering. When cutting started in the 1850s the major commodity was "square timber" for the British market. Muskoka's tallest, stoutest pines were cut and squared for use in shipbuilding and house construction. The trade soon shifted to lumber, suddenly in great demand in America's expanding west. When the railroads reached Muskoka in 1875, the demand grew even greater. By the 1880s, Gravenhurst alone had fourteen screeching sawmills. But even before the trains chugged on north, Muskoka was building boats.

For more than three centuries its native people had constructed

canoes. But when the settlers started swarming in far bigger craft were needed to speed families, supplies and livestock up the lakes. And so in 1866 Muskoka's Big Boat era began with the launching of entrepreneur A.P. Cockburn's first steamer, the *Wenonah*. Then, after the Port Carling locks were built to connect lakes Muskoka and Rosseau, Muskoka's major waterways soon echoed to the whistle of a dozen big white steamboats. By the early 1900s, Cockburn's Muskoka Lakes Navigation Company had become the largest inland waterway steamboat line in Canada. At the peak of the great steamboat era, 140 steamers plied Muskoka's big three lakes alone, with another 50 cruising the waters of Huntsville and the Lake of Bays.

A marsh on the margins of Lake Simcoe.

Meanwhile, Muskoka's infant settlements had mushroomed. The first community, Severn Bridge, had only a store, hotel and three houses in 1860. The following year, Mickey McCabe opened a log tavern in Gravenhurst, while Bracebridge had a small brick tavern and store, a log house and two log huts. Within a decade, Bracebridge boasted churches, three hotels, sawmills, stores, a newspaper and free schools. Similarly, by 1874 Gravenhurst not only had its sixteen sawmills and expanding steamboat company, but also a beverage plant, carriage works, scores of stores and hotels, a town hall, newspaper and four churches - plus a posh cricket club. In the same booming era, Huntsville had grown from a single dwelling to a thriving town with its own post office. And, as settlers swept in, the villages of Port Carling, Bala, Baysville, Beaumaris, Port Sydney, Utterson, Dwight and Ilfracombe also developed.

Yet ironically, while Muskoka's rocky terrain, craggy hills and dense forests spelled catastrophe for countless farmers, the same features comprised a bountiful lure for tourists - who today provide its major industry. Nearly 450,000 visitors pour in each summer.

The region, like any successful vacation area, required transportation services, proximity to a large urban population, hotels to accommodate families, businessmen active in promotion, a kindly climate and exquisite scenery. These prerequisites, as one Muskoka writer points out, are known as the four A's: attractions, accessibility, accommodations and advertising. By the mid-1860s, Muskoka boasted them all - plus hunting and fishing, and the beauty of its waters. Soon scores of Toronto holiday-seekers began riding in comfort on the Northern Railroad to Lake Simcoe, then on to Muskoka by stage and boat. At the same time adventurous Americans, hearing of the profusion of Muskoka's lakes, fish and game, started streaming in via Niagara Falls and Toronto. Even the Governor-General Lord Dufferin and his Lady made a pilgrimage to the new northern playground in 1874. They sailed from Gravenhurst to Bracebridge where bands and cheering crowds hailed their ride through town in the vice-regal carriage.

A decade later, when the railroad reached Bracebridge, the floodgates of tourism were opened wide. The great resort hotels began springing up. Rich businessmen from Ontario, Ohio and Pennsylvania began erecting the huge summer mansions which equalled or surpassed even those on the St. Lawrence.

Muskoka's fame as quintessential Cottage Country had begun.

*Huge rocks, tossed
and broken over
geological eons, line
the margins of
Georgian Bay.*

The white picket fence makes a traditional backdrop for lilies and black-eyed Susans.

Previous pages:
A colourful sky and calm water are balm to the spirit.

Summer's flowering effulgence in Beaumaris, Muskoka.

For some, the rugged north shore of Lake Superior is a wilderness of incomparable beauty.

The path to the boathouse, near Port Sandfield.

For some owners, as for this one on Georgian Bay, the cottage offers contact with nature in a wild mood.

*Northern Ontario -
in this case, a lake in
the vicinity of White
River - offers much
to the outdoors
enthusiast.*

*Sunset over Lake
Muskoka.*

Encumbering clothing lies abandoned on the rocks of Picnic Island, Georgian Bay.

Following pages:
Tiny islands are the summer residence of cottagers in Georgian Bay.

Lodges in the Wilderness

Provision is also made for winter visitors.

For four golden decades, from the 1880s through the 1920s, Muskoka was renowned for its grand resorts. At its peak it boasted nearly sixty that could be labelled posh, plus another eighty-five inns and hotels of distinguished summertime stature. Some of them lasted a century; a few still exist - and thrive. But sadly, most died in overnight infernos, of hard times especially in the Depression, or from old age.

The first Muskoka inn with accommodation was a rustic log tavern in Severn Bridge built by H.W. Dillon in 1860. Its patrons were mostly lumbermen, settlers and surveyors. The second was Mickey McCabe's Freemason's Arms Hotel in Gravenhurst, which he opened in 1861. The same year Hiram Macdonald built a hotel-tavern beneath the foaming Bracebridge falls. Eight years later another log hostel, the Polar Star Hotel, was erected in Port Carling above the new locks then being built.

But the father of Muskoka's true resorts was the New York entrepreneur William Pratt. Lured to Muskoka in 1869 by the dynamic A.P. Cockburn for a tour of the lakes on his steamers, the visionary Pratt bought a lofty piece of land where Rosseau village now stands. The only other inn in the area was the Humphrey Hotel, built in 1869, which provided accommodations for stagecoach travellers on the road to Parry Sound. Yet Pratt envisioned the area as a sportsman's paradise and set about building an ornate, verandahed three-storey showpiece. When the Rosseau House opened in 1870, it was Canada's first real wilderness resort. Although it took two days to reach it from Toronto, Pratt charged an outrageous five dollars a day. But this was the era of frock coats and hoopskirts, and the wealthy loved the place for its hunting, fishing, boating, lawn-bowling and dancing after dark.

The Rosseau House not only made the wilderness fashionable, but also dominated Muskoka's tourist scene for a decade - until one dawn in October, 1883, when it burst into flames and burned to the ground. Pratt never rebuilt, but his grand hotel set the pattern for all that followed. And they followed fast. The year after Rosseau House went up, A.P. Cockburn took another friend to Muskoka - Brampton merchant Hamilton Fraser. He, too, bought land at the head of Lake Joseph and built an even grander resort called The Summit House. Besides rooms for 250 guests, Fraser added a ballroom, acetylene lighting, a septic system, golf course, forty-seven-foot steam launch, the *Onaganoh*, and even a church and post office - which he named Port Cockburn. The Summit House flourished until 1915, when it too was gutted by fire.

But by the end of the 1880s, many of Muskoka's most famous resorts were running: Clevelands House, Ferndale House, Monteith House, Maplehurst Hotel, Prospect House, Beaumaris Hotel, Milford Bay House, Windermere House. And the Grand Old Ladies soon followed: Elgin House, Milford Manor, Rossclair Hotel, Belmont House, Pine Lands House, and the grandest of them all, The Royal Muskoka - Canada's first luxury summer resort. Built for $150,000 by the architect who designed the Waldorf Astoria, it held 350 guests and boasted steam heat, hot and cold running water, electric lights, plus tennis courts, bowling greens and golf course on its 130 sprawling acres. Then, in May 1952, it also lit Muskoka's night sky with flames.

The peak of the golden era ran from the mid-1890s to the start of the

A turn-of-the-century summer residence on Lake Muskoka.

First World War. At the beginning of that period, Muskoka boasted thirty resort hotels. By 1909 there were seventy-six on Lakes Muskoka, Rosseau and Joseph alone, holding up to 50,000 guests at one time. And during that massive building boom, the great Muskoka cottages were also going up.

The first real summer residents were two youths from Toronto, James Bain and John Campbell who, in July 1860, decided to holiday among the Muskoka settlers. Taking the train to Lake Simcoe and a steamboat to Orillia, they rowed the twelve miles to Severn Bridge where they stayed the night in Dillon's log tavern. The next day they walked to the present site of Gravenhurst, and pitched their tent. Each summer therafter they returned, bringing friends. In 1864 they formed the Muskoka Club and built cottages and a clubhouse on Lake Joseph's Yoho Island. By 1870 the club had fifty members. Meanwhile two Americans, H.P. Dwight and Erastus Wiman, had made fishing trips to the Lake of Bays where they established the Dwight-Wiman Sporting Club. And soon the rich and famous followed.

Orville Wright, the father of flight, owned an island in Muskoka which he reached on his thirty-two-foot launch, *Kitty Hawk*. Oscar Wilde sailed from Gravenhurst with Lord Alfred Douglas to visit the Marquess of Queensburry's lodge, and even King Edward VIII made the pilgrimage north. Department store tycoon Timothy Eaton built a huge summer home near Port Carling, while further up Lake Rosseau U.S. President Woodrow Wilson owned an island which he spoke of on his deathbed. *New Yorker* magazine writer E.B. White had a boys' camp near Dorset where his friend James Thurber went to sketch, while publishers Charles Musson and Jack McClelland had cottages nearby - the latter entertaining, with dry wit and martinis, such Canadian literati as Pierre Berton, Farley Mowat, Mordecai Richler, Leonard Cohen and artist Harold Town.

The Muskoka mansions, many of which still exist, were magnificent. They featured gabled windows above sweeping verandahs, a dozen rooms for servants alone, miniature railroads, elevators rising from the docks to the hilltop homes above, and huge cedar boathouses built to house small fleets. But most of the summer palaces, like the old Victorian resorts and great white steamboats, were made of wood. They were suseptible to rot, age and sudden infernos which all caused devastation. The golden era couldn't last.

The Depression took its toll. And so did both world wars. In the fifteen years after 1930, thirty-one hotels disappeared. Since 1945, another thirty-eight have died. Also, in the past four decades, every Muskoka steamboat sank, burned or ran aground - save one. In 1983, the S.S. *Segwun* was miraculously restored to service, and sails on today, the unquestioned Queen of the Muskoka Lakes. She's the oldest passenger-carrying steamship still sailing in North America.

And, while the *Segwun* returned like a phoenix, so has Muskoka's tourism. During the post-war era, with the advent of inexpensive package tours and jet travel to Europe and the Caribbean, it appeared that Muskoka's resorts would vanish. But suddenly the Yuppies, growing jaded with Club Meds and islands-in-the-sun, are rediscovering the beauties of the north. The remaining resorts are enjoying a resurgence of business. Inns with such nostalgic names as Clevelands, Elgin, Paignton and Windermere House, as well as Deerhurst and Muskoka Sands, are today not only thriving, but also expanding. Like the S.S. *Segwun*, they are rising from the ashes of the past.

Roches Point, Lake Simcoe: traditionally a prestigious location for a summer residence.

*For most cottagers,
the lake or river is the
attraction - a source
of unending
fascination.*

Cottage country is not limited to Ontario. This cottage is situated on Bowen Island, off the southern coast of British Columbia.

Following pages: Chairs made of sprung wrought iron in a sun motif shine on a lawn on Lake Simcoe.

A canoe house, slide,
diving platform and
boathouse - all water
sports provided for -
on Lake Rosseau.

A fabulously fanciful boathouse with a circular veranda.

The supplier of paint in Ontario's cottage country needed to stock just one colour in quantity: white.

Elm wood, now scarce because of Dutch elm disease, has generally been the favoured material for springboards.

Not all cottages are situated on lakefronts. The hills, forests and fields near King Township provide peace and seclusion for this modern summer home.

*The bridge leads to a
teahouse in a private
cottage property in
the Thousand Islands.*

Part of a miniature village lovingly constructed on a tiny island in Lake Muskoka.

A traditional log cottage on Lake Rosseau.

Every part of the cottage, including the wide door, is an original, hand-wrought creation.

*A splendidly-
maintained older
dwelling on Lake
Rosseau.*

An Ontario gothic tradition is given expression in this waterfront property near Brockville.

Everywhere throughout the short, brilliant summer of cottage country, people grow flowers in pots, planters and flowerbeds.

A grocery store in every cottage community sells ice cream, stamps and other staples.

Following pages: Contemplative pursuits for long summer evenings: music and literature.

Ideally, the cottage resident takes housecleaning tasks lightly. The broom is handy to push aside the day's accumulation of sand.

*The cottage is
comforting partly
because, from one
year to the next, it
remains unchanged.*

A massive stone
lintel, and a mantel of
granite, make an
elemental fireplace in
a cottage on Lake
Rosseau.

The picture window, bringing the view of the woods and lake into the living room, changed cottage construction in the 1950s and succeeding decades.

Perhaps the essence of the cottage: the screened-in porch.

Decorations expelled from the house in the city find their way into the cottage where they remain indefinitely.

The little library is an amenity essential to any cottage.

*Primitive and modern
ways to get around in
water: birchbark
canoe and gleaming
mahogany launches.*

There's room in the boathouse for smaller craft, too.

A home within earshot of water lapping against the dock, on Lake Joseph.

The steeply-pitched roof is a necessary defence against winter snow which, on a flatter surface, could accumulate to a dangerously weighty depth.

*Two-storey
boathouses conflict
with modern
building codes, but
older ones can be
maintained.*

The boathouse was usually constructed by local craftsmen in winter on a frozen lake.

The room above the boathouse provided space for games and the storage of equipment.

The "porthole" windows lend a nautical air to this boathouse and canoe house.

The weathered facade of a Victorian boathouse on Lake Simcoe.

Lumber and carpenters were both more readily available when structures such as this boathouse on Lake Joseph were built.

*A substantial canoe
house in Beaumaris,
Muskoka.*

Obviously this boathouse provides more than shelter for boats - it is a summer recreation complex.

On a summer's evening, a few decades ago, the dock might have been lined with launches, with a party in progress upstairs.

A splendidly simple, symmetrical cottage in Honey Harbor, Georgian Bay.

*A traditional cottage
and boathouse
caught between
contemporary
structures on the St.
Lawrence River, near
Gananoque.*

Bridges and stairs connect boathouse and cottage to the lakefront in Muskoka.

Not so much a cottage as a summer home, buildings like this housed the larger families of an earlier age for the entire summer.

Elaborate latticework like this was unfashionable for a while, but is regaining popularity.

The windowbox overflowing with flowers ensures that little sunlight filters into the gloomy boathouse.

The bollard on the dock harks back to the era when steam launches were regularly made fast to the side.

The simplicity of this front porch on the Quebec portion of the St. Lawrence contrasts with the more elaborate carpentry typical of traditional Ontario cottages.

Part of the casual character of traditional cottage country derives from the locally made stick furniture.

Idle Pursuits

A gentle twilight breeze wafts in through the bathroom window.

To its natives, tourists and cottagers, Muskoka has always been a place of sporting pastimes. Its wild game and fighting fish have lured outdoorsmen for decades. In the early days they portaged in by canoe, or took one of Cockburn's steamboats. After the First World War, hundreds more flew in on the air service run by the great Canadian war ace, Billy Bishop. But the region has also been famous for myriad pursuits.

In the 1880s, William Lyon Mackenzie King sailed up in the summers to play with the Beaumaris cricket side. American steel magnate Andrew Carnegie sailed his steamer *Phoebe* on Lake Muskoka, while Timothy Eaton raced Canada's fastest yacht at Windermere - the resort where marathon swimmer Cindy Nicholas later trained. Even Clark Gable and Carole Lombard spent trysts in Muskoka playing tennis.

Others went north for more artistic pursuits. Group of Seven artists A.Y. Jackson, Arthur Lismer, J.E.H. MacDonald and their pal Tom Thomson all painted throughout Muskoka. Jackson's old colleague John Rennie still paints from his Port Carling studio. Lucy Maud Montgomery wrote a novel, *The Blue Castle*, about Muskoka during one of her summers there, while the famed Mohawk poet Pauline Johnson wrote a lengthy ode to "the lakeland... where the April suns are gold."

For cottagers craving artistic pleasures themselves, Muskoka has provided amenities in abundance. Live theatre first became prominent in 1934 when the John Holden Players opened their initial season in Bala - the first Canadian stock theatre in English Canada. Followed in 1948 by Donald and Murray Davis's Straw Hat Players, the troupe entranced packed houses each summer in both Gravenhurst and Port Carling.

In 1973, this succession of companies finally evolved into the Muskoka Festival, becoming not only Ontario's third largest summer theatre festival (after Stratford and Shaw), but also Canada's oldest professional summer theatre. The actors who began with the company include Barbara Hamilton, Araby Lockhart, Andrea Martin, William Hutt, Gordon Pinsent, Helen Shaver and a prop-builder named Donald Sutherland.

Meanwhile tiny Bala was establishing a tradition of its own as the greatest names of the Big Band era jammed them in at Dunne's Pavilion ("Where All Muskoka Dances"). Crowds of 2,000 paid admission while hundreds more listened from boat decks as Glen Miller, Louis Armstrong, Tommy and Jimmy Dorsey, Cab Calloway, Woody Herman, Count Basie and Duke Ellington rocked the village.

Today, like the wondrous tuba-thumping orchestra that once belted Tipperary from the stern of the S.S. *Sagamo* on its Hundred Mile Cruise, the Big Bands have echoed into history. The Muskoka Festival, however, not only survives but thrives - as do many of the superb mahogany yachts which once made Muskoka world-famous. Today the boats live on in Port Carling's antique boat show which attracts thousands each August.

But their origin is legend. Gravenhurst achieved international fame not only as the birthplace of both the great white steamboats and Dr. Norman Bethune, China's surgical supersaint, but also as the home of the renowned Greavette and Ditchburn speedboats which set international records.

The four Ditchburn brothers epitomize Muskoka's pioneering history. Arriving from England in 1869, they started by building rowboats in their attic for William Pratt's Rosseau House. After the resort was gutted, the

In pursuit of panfish from dockside.

Ditchburn boatworks was established in Gravenhurst, and soon had lucrative branches and marinas throughout the lakes. In 1913, a Ditchburn speedboat ran a twenty-four-hour trial on Lake Rosseau, stopping only for gas and a new crew, and the next year set a world record for distance travelled by a boat under any kind of power. Then the world's finest luxury yachts began coming from the Ditchburn dock, such as Sir John Eaton's *Kawandag* and Col. T. Duff's elegant *Idlize*.

During the First World War, the British Navy commissioned the company to build the powerful "crash boats" which rescued downed pilots in the channel. Then for years Ditchburn's speedboats won innumerable gold cups in Detroit's famed international races, with such designs as the superb Estelle series. But the company concentrated solely on luxury craft, and the 1929 financial market crash wiped it out.

Yet while the Depression sank Ditchburn, it proved to be a bonanza to the fledgling Greavette Boat Works of Gravenhurst. Its founder, Tom Greavette, who once worked for Ditchburn, started production in 1930 with his innovative "non-pound" keels, and soon his exquisite Streamliner models were selling internationally. Then, after building the deadly 112-foot-long Fairmile patrol cruisers in the Second World War, Greavette became even more celebrated for its Miss Canada speedboats with their thrusting Rolls-Royce engines.

Meanwhile in Port Carling, the Johnston boatworks had been turning out twenty-seven-foot launches since the turn of the century. And in 1916, William Johnston made boating history with his invention of the Disappearing Propellor, an inexpensive rowboat-shaped craft with a shifting inboard prop, which sold internationally - and is still a collector's item. In 1925, Johnston also started the Port Carling Boat Works which produced the hugely popular Seabird inboards. By then two other local boatworks, Duke's and Matheson's, were producing coveted launches. During the Second World War, Duke's built nine Fairmiles for the navy; Port Carling Boat Works made four Fairmiles plus two minesweepers; and Johnston's plant alone turned out fifty-eight whale boats. In fact, from its boom years until 1968, Port Carling's master boat builders produced more than 2,000 motor craft - a record unequalled in Canada.

Hundreds of these splendid craft still purr from gingerbread boathouses to ply Muskoka's lakes. They carry the summer residents of Muskoka's 20,000 cottages to Gravenhurst's old Opera House, Norman Bethune's birthplace, the Music on the Barge weekend concerts, and the *Segwun* dock for sunset dinner cruises; to Bala's Cranberry Festival beside the falls; Huntsville's Pioneer Village with its century-old buildings; Bracebridge's annual Antique Show, the Lady Muskoka wharf and Santa's Village; to Port Carling's Pioneer Museum, Antique Boat Show and summer theatre. The cottagers still skim by yacht to Muskoka's sailing regattas (held since 1894), its weekly waterski shows and autumn Cavalcades of Colour, to its scores of tennis courts, fourteen golf courses and fifty-three churches.

The summertime people swim, sail, ski and fish in its waters and picnic beside its shores. They breathe fresh pine, old cedar and barbecue smoke. They hear the creak of oarlocks and snapping sails in the wind.

All are idle, but sweet, pursuits - found only in those places we call Cottage Country.

A waterskier awaits takeoff.

*The canoe tradition
has endured through
the years, adapting to
different uses and
circumstances.*

A Greavette
Streamliner - an
antique launch
constructed by a
Gravenhurst firm of
boatbuilders.

*Duke Boats on the
Indian River, Port
Carling.*

Sailing off the north shore of Manitoulin Island.

*Sunfish sailboats on
a dock on Lake
Joseph.*

*Flat-bottomed boats
provide stability for
members of the
Caledon Trout Club.*

The lateen sail and leeboard propel the canoe with a minimum of human effort and maximum stability on a summer evening.

*Antique launches
lovingly polished to a
piano-like finish.*

A boat with inboard motor and disappearing propeller (the lever is used to reset the propeller) beside a vintage rowboat.

*Keeping - cherishing -
antique mahogany
launches, many
locally built, is a
Muskoka tradition.*

The launch and log boathouse are of the same era.

The disappearing propeller, or Dispro, a mechanism that allowed the propeller to be pushed into a channel in the hull of the boat, was the invention of a Port Carling firm of boat builders.

*Boats on a dock on
Lake Joseph.*

The marine railway at Big Chute, Muskoka, performs the same function as canal locks.

A bass-fishing derby in Georgian Bay attracts competitors from all over the continent.

*A member of the
Caledon Trout Club
stalks his prey.*

*The sun browns skin
and blisters paint at a
cottage on the St.
Lawrence.*

Casual barbecues are a universal aspect of the contemporary cottage scene.

No better perch for sunbathers than a shelf of sun-warmed rocks with cool water a turn away.

Regatta on Lake Muskoka.

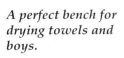

A perfect bench for drying towels and boys.

*The essential
implements of
summer camp
activities: life jackets
and paddles.*

*Boat replaces bike for
the boy who delivers
the newspaper on
Lake Muskoka.*

Swimming togs draped where they are most likely to dry.

Bedtime delayed.